Fridays
With Ms. Mélange: Haiti

Jenny Delacruz

Illustrations by Danko Herrera

Printed in the United States of America

First Edition, 2019

ISBN: 978-1-7342219-0-9 Paperback

ISBN: 978-1-7342219-2-3 Hardcover

ISBN: 978-1-7342219-1-6 eBook

This book is dedicated to my husband,
Joseph, and our two sons, Joey and James.

This is Nia. She loves to learn and explore. Today, she's going to learn an important story in world history.

Nia rushed to school because...

...all the 6th graders looked forward to seeing Ms. Mélange.

She teaches history and current events every Friday.

On this Friday, Ms. Mélange had placed a napkin with a cube of sugar and a grape on each desk.

Ms. Mélange asked, "Which is sweeter?"

Leoh said, "The sugar."

"Great! Eat the sugar cube first and then the grape," Ms. Mélange instructed.

Leoh whined, "Ew. My grape is sour!"

Ms. Mélange said, "On its own, the grape is sweet, but it tastes sour compared to the sweetness of the sugar. Today, we're going to explore how this analogy relates to the history of Haiti. Does anyone know what an **analogy** is?"

Emma asked, "Is an analogy like a clever way of comparing two ideas?"

"Haiti was the first free Black republic and the only nation to form after a successful slave revolution," said Jean.

"Correct. But sadly, it is now one of the most exploited, and as a result, poorest countries in the western world. In our analogy, the sugar represents the successful revolution. Now think about what the grape, by itself, represents and what the sour taste of the grape after eating the sugar represents."

Maybe the grape is freedom? Freedom is sweet too, right? I get it! The sourness of the grape represents Haiti's **exploitation** after gaining freedom. The sour after the sweet!

"Does anyone know where Haiti is?" Ms. Mélange asked.

Jean answered, "In the Caribbean!"

"Yes! It's on the western end of the island of Hispaniola. Jean, your parents are from Haiti, aren't they?"

"Yeah. We speak French and Haitian Creole," Jean said.

Haitian Creole is a mix of French, West African, Taíno, Spanish, and Portuguese.

Ms. Mélange said, "Christopher Columbus landed on the island in 1492 and named it Hispaniola, or little Spain. A group of people called the Taíno were already living there when Columbus arrived."

"Before Columbus came, the Taíno also lived in Cuba, Jamaica, and Puerto Rico. Unfortunately, the Europeans killed about three million Taíno when they colonized the islands," said Ms. Mélange.

"Isn't that **genocide**?" Leoh asked.

"You are correct," said Ms. Mélange.

Ms. Mélange responded, "The Taíno did nothing wrong, Scarlett. They simply had resources other countries wanted. Countless Taíno starved to death because they were forced to work in the mines rather than work their farms. The Taíno who survived became slaves, just like the Africans of the **transatlantic slave trade**."

Just like my Native American ancestors, they also died from diseases the Europeans brought with them, like the flu and smallpox. Even more died fighting the Europeans.

"As the Spanish ships traveled home with their valuable cargo of gold, copper, and crops, French pirates seized some of the Spanish vessels and robbed them," Ms. Mélange said.

"From then on, the Spanish and French fought constantly," Ms. Mélange continued. "Eventually, in 1697, Spain and France signed a treaty to end the fighting. France claimed the western part of Hispaniola and called it Saint Domingue, while the Spanish claimed the eastern part and called it Santo Domingo."

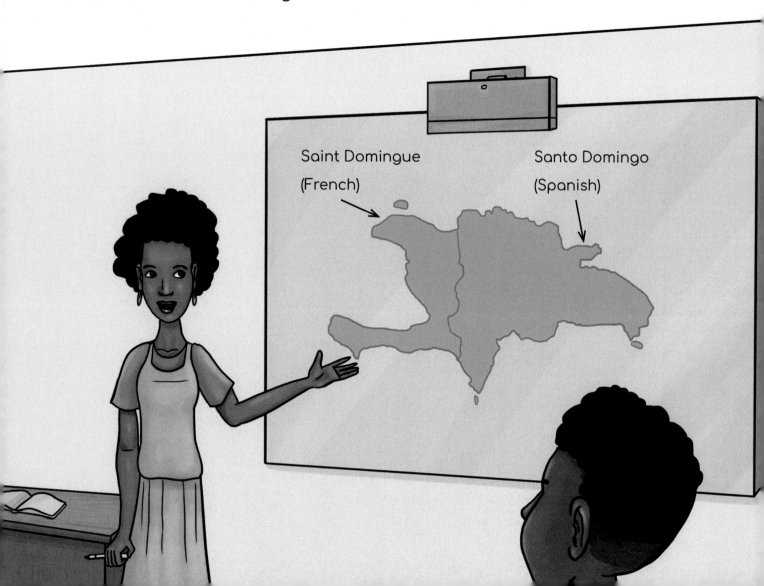

"Does anyone know what the sad source of France's wealth was then?" asked Ms. Mélange.

"Was it slavery?" asked Nia.

"Correct, Nia. France was active in the transatlantic slave trade. Many African slaves died within three years of capture due to the cruel plantation system in Saint Domingue. Those that died were simply replaced with more Africans. But once in a while, a rare few purchased their freedom and became known as free Blacks or free people of color,"

Jean said, "L'Ouverture led the slaves and free people of color when they declared their freedom from slavery, right?"

"Right, Jean. By 1791, the slaves and free Blacks finally felt hope when Toussaint L'Ouverture, a former slave, formed an army in a successful revolution against the French. However, it didn't end well for him," Ms. Mélange said.

Didn't something terrible happen to him?

"That's right, Jean. In 1802, Napoleon Bonaparte, a French general, tricked and arrested L'Ouverture, who then died in prison."

Ms. Mélange replied, "The slaves and free people of color didn't give up. They rose up again under a new leader, Jean-Jacques Dessalines."

"The army fought against France, Spain, and England for 12 long years. Dessalines finally declared independence on January 1, 1804, and changed the country's name to Haiti. Haiti was the original Taíno name for the island, and it means 'land of high mountains,'" explained Ms. Mélange.

Ms. Mélange said, "That's a great question, Nia. For one, the slaves and the free Blacks outnumbered the French on the island. This gave them an advantage."

Nia jumped in, "But 12 years is a really long time!"

"You're right, Nia. It's about as long as you've all been alive," Ms. Mélange agreed. "But another reason they had the courage to keep fighting was because even though most of them were slaves, they had held on tightly to their African and Taíno roots. They remembered who they were, so they could unite. They came together and kept fighting because their shared identity was so strong."

"After Haiti became independent, Dessalines wrote the country's first constitution. It was the first in the world to recognize that all people are created equal despite their race. It was **revolutionary** because it granted freedom to any slave from anywhere in the world that arrived on the shores of Haiti," the teacher explained.

Today, Nia learned that our self-identity and connection to our roots are so powerful it can impact not only the course of our lives but also that of generations to come.

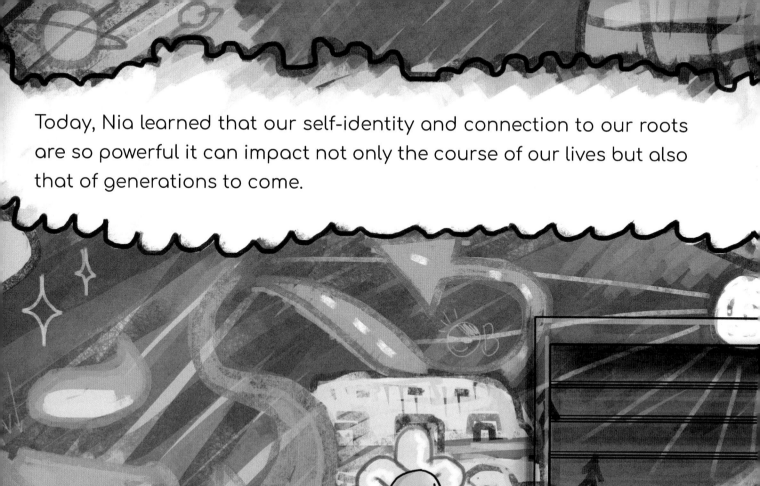

Questions for Reflection

1. What part of the story stood out to you?

2. What questions do you still have?

3. How did you feel about the story and why?

Glossary

Analogy: a comparison of two things based on a similar aspect

Exploit: to unfairly use for one's advantage

Genocide: the deliberate and systematic destruction of a racial, political, or cultural group

Revolutionary: causing or bringing about a significant or fundamental change

Transatlantic slave trade: a segment of the global slave trade that transported between 10 and 12 million Africans across the Atlantic Ocean to the Americas from the 16th to the 19th century

Sources

Abdul, R. (2016). "Taíno: Indigenous Caribbeans." *Black History 365*. Retrieved from https://www.blackhistorymonth.org.uk/article/section/pre-colonial-history/Taíno-indigenous-caribbeans/

Baptiste, N. (2014). "Terror, Repression, and Diaspora: The Baby Doc Legacy." *Foreign Policy in Focus*. Retrieved from

Farmer, Paul. (2011). *Haiti after the earthquake*. New York, NY: Public Affairs.

Gaffield, J. (2015). *Haitian Connections in the Atlantic World: Recognition After Revolution*. Chapel Hill, NC: University of North Carolina Press.

Gates, H. L., Hewes, J., Grant, W., & Pollack, R. (2001). *PBS Black in Latin America: Episode 1*. [DVD]. Inkwell Films/Wall to Wall Productions.

Genocide. (2019). Retrieved from https://www.britannica.com/

The International Trade Administration. (2019). "Haiti - Mining and Minerals." *Export.gov*. Retrieved from https://www.export.gov/article?id=Haiti-Mining-and-Minerals

Renda, M. A. (2004). *Taking Haiti: Military Occupation & the Culture of U.S. Imperialism, 1915-1940*. Chapel Hill, NC: University of North Carolina Press.

Shamsie, Y. & Thompson, A.S. (2006). *Haiti: Hope for a Fragile State*. Waterloo, Ontario: Wilfrid Laurier University Press.

Sidder, A. (2016). "How Cholera Spread So Quickly Through Haiti." *National Geographic*. Retrieved from https://news.nationalgeographic.com/2016/08/haiti-cholera-crisis-united-nations-admission/

Slavery and Remembrance: A Guide to Sites, Museums, and Memory. (2019). *Haiti (Saint-Domingue)*. Retrieved from http://slaveryandremembrance.org/articles/article/?id=A0111

About the Author

Jenny Delacruz's passion to teach her sons about world history and current events led to this unique series. Jenny is a philanthropist who advocates for human rights. A portion of the proceeds from this work will go towards supporting orphanages in Haiti. Visit us on YouTube at: Storytime with Ms. Mélange to watch us read this story out loud. There, you'll find other great stories with diverse characters by various authors and illustrators!

23273445R00024